Manifestes
2

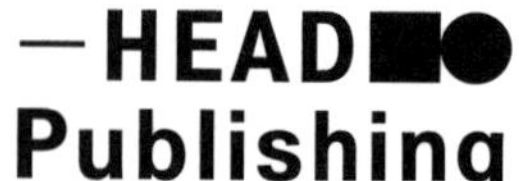

Nicolas Nova
Investigation/Design

The advent of design research has ushered in a new role for designers.[1] In addition to realizing projects—designing objects, clothing, interfaces, services, stage design—they could now produce knowledge as well. This phenomenon is due to two developments. The first is the overhaul of institutions of higher education in the wake of the Bologna Process in the early 2000s, which has prompted schools of art and design to develop research activities of an "academic" cast.[2] Meanwhile, designers and agencies have increasingly taken an interest in producing books and reports of all kinds, including academic articles, as

1   Given the multiple meanings of the term, I will be using the definition of the "designer" as a creative practitioner trained in the European tradition of the applied arts and working in product design, interface and digital interaction design, fashion design, architecture, graphic design or even service design. See also Potter, 2011

2   For an overview of the many issues involved in and debates on this subject, see e.g. the special issue of the journal *Hermès* (Renucci and Réol, 2015) or the book *Recherche-création en design* (Léchot-Hirt, 2010).

well as graphic displays of data, films, documents and interactive installations. This trend, which is much in evidence in the fields of art and architecture, has engendered a new form of research known as "practice-based research," which involves the production and use of artifacts—from posters to interactive devices, furniture and exhibitions—to promote the development or renewal of knowledge. The primary object of this approach for designers and artists is not to produce a work of art or design. Practice-based research and, consequently, the creative practices of the designers involved in such projects are not by any means confined to choosing a form for the knowledge thereby produced; they correspond to a unique kind of knowledge, one that is distinct from other academic disciplines.[3]

As a teacher at a school that trains students in design and design research, I have long wondered what might constitute a form of practice-based research in design: in other words, producing knowledge through the ways in which designers go about doing and understanding things, with a

3   "Artistic" or "creative research" *(recherche-création)* constitutes an epistemology, i.e. a knowledge production mode that has a coherence of its own (Findeli, 2003, 2010; Léchot-Hirt, 2010). Nigel Cross talks about "designerly ways of knowing" to refer to these ways of generating knowledge through practice (Cross, 2007). My aim in this book is to objectify this mode of production by describing designerly practice.
4   My description of a design researcher's approach here is based on the social sciences, which is but one of many possible bases; see e.g. Samuel Bianchini, 2017.

modicum of rigor. As a social anthropologist initially trained in the natural sciences, and in this sense accustomed to the exercise of describing the world and its actors, I have long felt that investigation is a point of convergence between all these disciplines and design. If designers can be researchers, that's partly owing to their ability to observe, analyze, describe and render—in other words, to produce a form of investigation. And this is the approach I will make a case for here in a few brief chapters that will elucidate my views, which have evolved over the course of various encounters and projects and are, above all, fueled by my teaching and research work over the past few years at the HEAD–Genève and elsewhere. I will begin by tracing the close connections between the practices of design and investigation to show how designers become investigators by combining established methods and their own *modi operandi*. Based on that exposition and some projects that serve as cases in point, I will go on to outline four aspects of design research that distinguish designers' investigations: the construction of a continually renewed process; an inclusive outlook that inclines them to spontaneously incorporate all sorts of different approaches and ideas; the importance of materiality in their investigative practice; and the importance of form in the rendering of their works.[4] I will then conclude with some thoughts about the future of design investigations.

INVESTIGATIVE DESIGNERS
Designers are becoming investigators, combining established methods with their own ways of doing things.

Designers are commonly viewed as creating objects characterized by a controlled aesthetic and emerging instantaneously from a keen imagination. But anyone who has spent some time in a designer's studio knows this is a far cry from the reality of design in practice, which involves spells of tortuous progress, immersion in the context of the intervention, the production of a multitude of intermediate objects such as diagrams, observational drawings, photographs and prototypes of all kinds,[5] in addition to making models and holding team meetings (with their share of endless discussions), alternating between moments of enthusiasm, discouragement and surprise—emotions often exponentially amplified by meetings with clients, who usually need to be convinced by showing them those intermediate objects.

5   An idea proposed by Dominique Vinck, a sociologist of science and technology, corresponding to the conception, production, negotiation and circulation of objects in various forms in order to understand collective action and the results thereof (Vinck, 2009, p. 53-54).

[Fig. 1] **Observational sketch of the movements involved in repairing a smartphone during a project investigating the durability of digital devices (Anaïs Bloch, 2020)**

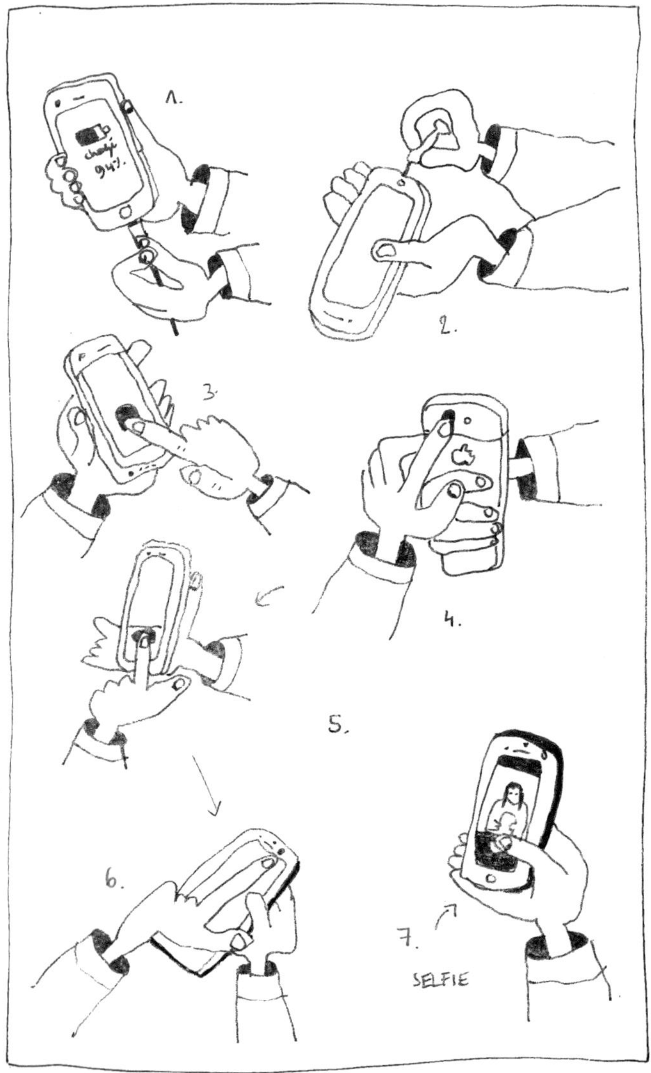

Observation is one method increasingly employed in the design professions, giving rise to a whole terminology that reflects its growing importance in the creative process. Terms like "preliminary research," "user research," "user experience research" and the simplistic generic "design research"[6] have caught on over the past thirty years. While these terms tend to change regularly, they do correspond to the idea of developing a creative project through a form of immersion in a social situation that involves individuals and their practices.[7] These stages of observation may also correspond to the use of such approaches along the way, e.g. testing prototypes on prospective users in order to identify their needs or the problems they encounter, to reorient the project or enrich the creative process with unique elements or inspiring references.[8]

6   "Design research" is reductive in the sense that the term is used by a whole community of designers as synonymous with what I am discussing here, though it actually refers more broadly to various forms of research on, by and for design, ranging from the history of a specific area of design or a specific object to preliminary studies to provide a creative framework or knowledge production by designers' creations (see Koskinen *et al.*, 2011).
7   Like architecture and engineering, design is a project-based discipline in the sense that this "unit of design work" (Vial, 2014, p. 17) "refers both to the sequence of actions required to produce a new artefact and the means usually used to represent the different stages of development of this artefact (sketches, drawings, plans, models, prototypes)" (Léchot-Hirt, 2010, p. 29). See also Findeli and Bousbaci, 2005.
8   For further details, see Nova, 2015.

Confrontation with reality is deemed so vital that it has become a professional specialty among designers at agencies, big companies and research and development laboratories. Job descriptions like "user researcher," "design researcher," and even "design ethnographer" each convey a certain vision of what design, research or observation is. They testify to the appropriation of methods from the social sciences, such as ethnographically inspired observation.[9] However, especially in the field of "interaction design," they can also be quantitative techniques that may involve the use of questionnaires or the analysis of digital footprints, for example.[10] Depending on the designer's training and background, these investigations

9   An appropriation whose genealogy can be traced in the stages by which empirical approaches have spread from the humanities and social sciences to design. Ethnography has been used by designers since the mid-1990s, particularly in the field of computer science and human-machine interfaces, after the positivist approaches of psychology and cognitive ergonomics widely used from the 1980s on (cf. Nova, 2014, p. 29-45).

10   The statistical survey, which is rarely used by designers, is catching on in the wake of the growing interest in digital traces (Big Data), which are accessible via online platforms and can give rise to multiple analyses and visual representations. The latter are useful in guiding action and decision-making, especially in the fields of digital and service design.

11   For an analysis of the investigative designer's counterpart in the field of art, the "artist as ethnographer", see e.g. Foster, 1996, and a recent reinterpretation thereof (Duperrex, 2019).

12   It is found in certain sub-communities of practice, however, like the term "contextual inquiry" in HMI and digital design.

                     Investigation/Design

are often pieced together from miscellaneous concepts, framing elements, methods and tactics drawn from such disciplines as anthropology, sociology, experimental psychology and ergonomics. This approach is often combined with spontaneous personal initiatives and diverse artistic practices, given the permeability of the teachings and cultures of art and applied arts.

These various ways of investigating the world, by or for designers' projects, correspond to the emergence of a new figure: that of the investigative designer.[11] This approach is catching on, for, besides the new professions it has spawned, it has also become an end in itself for certain designers who are interested in producing publications in unique and original formats, from solidly textual monographs and coffee-table books to fanzines, blog posts, newsletters and exhibitions that draw abundantly on material produced and analyzed in their investigations.

While designers themselves seldom use the term "investigation",[12] it strikes me as an illuminating way of putting it in order to convey a sense of the various phases involved: observation, analysis of the material produced during investigation, and presentation or rendering thereof in the form of artifacts of various kinds. When interaction designers immerse themselves for weeks at a time in, say, the lives of music-streaming platform users in order to document and comprehend their practices and then redesign the interface or the recommendation mechanisms, how can we

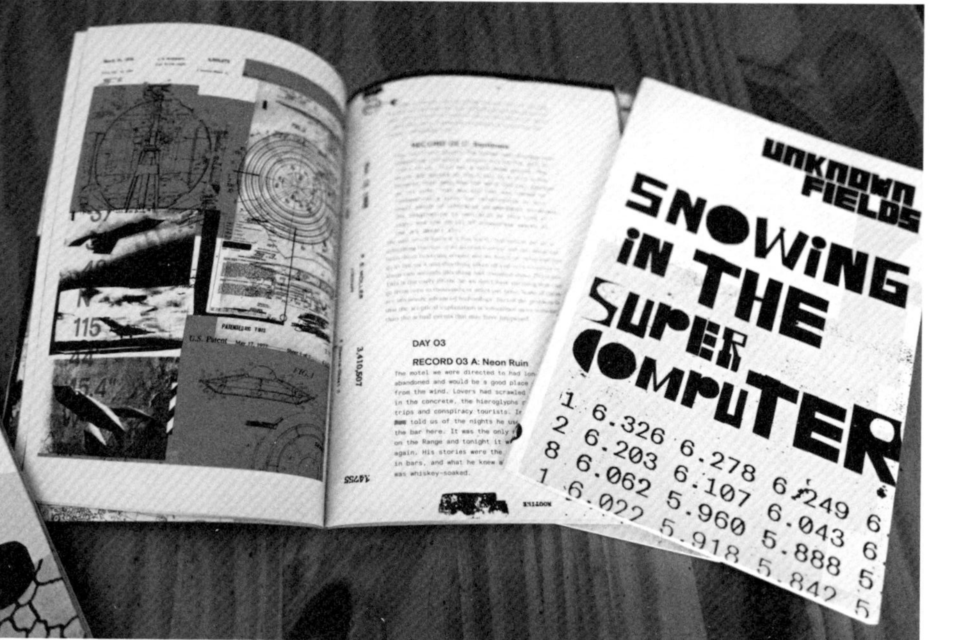

DAY 03

RECORD 03 A: Neon Ruin

The motel we were directed to had lon
abandoned and would be a good place
from the wind. Lovers had scrawled
in the concrete, the hieroglyphs
trips and conspiracy tourists. Ir
told us of the nights he us
the bar here. It was the only
on the Range and tonight it w
again. His stories were the
in bars, and what he knew
was whiskey-soaked.

not regard this as a form of investigation? Even if their efforts don't necessarily culminate in the publication of an academic article, the designers are likely to produce multiple documents that will be useful in the creation of interfaces: diagrams and displays to present the information gathered and their findings, as well as reports on their experiences. And what about a design agency commissioned by a museum to study animal movements in urban environments and come up with a way to display their findings? Similarly, when the members of a graphic design studio engage in observation sessions by day and by night as well as random interviews of passers-by, immersing themselves for years in the uses of street furniture and all the elements that compose the texture of contemporary cities, and then put out a book providing systematic documentation of the tensions, frictions and disturbances they encountered in public spaces, isn't this an investigation too?

Admittedly, these investigations often take place in a commercial context. Admittedly, they are often based on a conceptual and methodological framework that is more spontaneous than systematic. And admittedly, many of these projects never get beyond the stage of collecting or compiling observations and are not always put into perspective by means of a conceptual framework, an in-depth analysis or a clear-cut description of what they have to add to previous

[Fig. 2] A series of booklets produced on the basis of field surveys by Unknown Field Division, a nomadic collective studio for design research (2016)

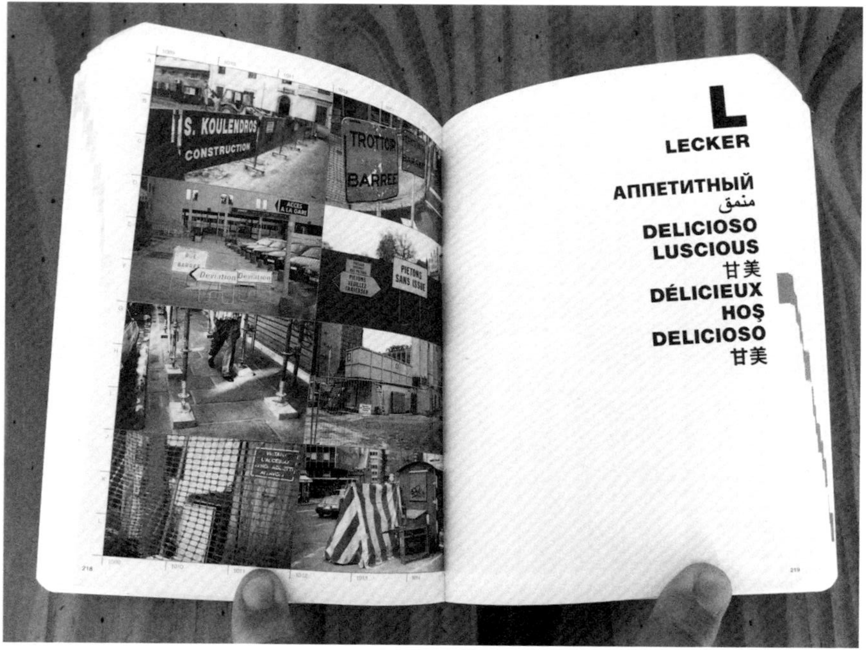

L

LECKER

АППЕТИТНЫЙ

منمق

DELICIOSO
LUSCIOUS
甘美
DÉLICIEUX
HOŞ
DELICIOSO
甘美

work carried out by their peers. And yet, these investigations yield a profusion of more or less analytical documents, maps and portraits reflecting important issues in the lives of the individuals encountered in the process; issues that are shared with the creative investigating team. An investigation may be carried out as a preliminary to the creation of a given product, or its goal may be to create knowledge and skills, but in either case it is indeed an investigation. Without attempting an intellectual genealogy here,[13] let us recall that, in the academic context of the social sciences, the term "investigation" refers to a general approach to understanding the world based on a framework comprising the following four elements (Berthelot, 2001; Olivier de Sardan, 2008):

- The clarification of a specific approach, which may be linked to the research context (producing knowledge in general or action-oriented knowledge as in the case of applied research).
- The construction of a topic, a subject to be researched and studied (a social practice, a technical object, a specific context),

13 A genealogy which would show that, besides ethnographic investigation in social and cultural anthropology, this term intersects with and takes up several intellectual traditions, such as pragmatic philosophy (John Dewey's logic and theory of inquiry) and the Chicago School's social investigation (at the interface between sociology and journalism), but also police investigation and its so-called "indiciary paradigm" (Ginzburg, 1979; Boltanski, 2012).

based on a question, problem or issue to be resolved.

- A rigorous method of apprehension (methodology) that involves researchers working, for a more or less extended period of time, as closely as possible to the "natural situations" of the subjects of the investigation, in their daily lives, habits, relations to everyday objects, and their conversations, in order to produce clearly situated, contextualized knowledge that takes into account the subjects' practices, their day-to-day representations and the meaning they ascribe to the situations they experience.
- Presentation of findings, which, in the social sciences, generally takes written form.

The three examples of investigative designers given above involve a number of conceptual and methodological choices with respect to these four points. Their position is clear since their aim is to produce factual or action-oriented knowledge (Point 1); they construct a topic of study oriented towards specific questions and towards describing situations, practices and sometimes the meaning that people ascribe to them, through subject-matter like the presence of animals in urban environments, streaming platforms and urban space (Point 2); they establish an investigation protocol adapted to their objective, their questions and their subject (Point 3); and they produce various forms of presentation, generally to be shared more or less publicly, which they may be called upon to explain or take as a basis for decision-making (Point 4). In other words, the research activities of investigative designers can be described as variations on social science investigations. These four components necessitate choices and approaches that are at once close to and distinct from those taken by sociologists and anthropologists.

Thus, the designer can be an investigator. While this position may well involve a dual approach to the world, namely seeking to understand it and intervening in it,[14] it is a matter of investigation all the same. Having established this close connection between design and investigation, we may now turn to the question of what is special about the way designers go about it. In other words, what are the investigative methods and forms peculiar to designers, and do they shed any light on the potential for projects at the intersection between the social sciences and prac-

14   As Herbert Simon put it in 1969: "To design is to devise courses of action aimed at changing existing situations into preferred ones" (Simon, 1969, p. 111). Or, in Alain Findeli's phrase, "to improve or at least maintain the habitability of the world" (Findeli, 2010, p. 292). Or, as Tim Ingold defines it, design, paired with anthropology, is a transformative practice: "The observations, descriptions and propositions of design anthropology are not retrospective but prospective: their purpose is not to interpret but to transform. Design, in short, is not and cannot be a practice of ethnography; it is rather an alternative way to ethnography of doing anthropology—a way that releases the speculative and experimental possibilities of the discipline that the traditional appeal to ethnography has suppressed" (Ingold, 2014, p. 6).

tice-based research? To answer these questions, I'm going to describe four components that strike me as being unique and remarkable, and illustrate them by referring to projects I have come across over the past fifteen years of teaching and research at the intersection between ethnography and design.

Designers are unique investigators in terms
of their focus on constructing, assembling and
reinventing processes.

Like all other designers, investigative designers make use of a working process that they transform or reinvent for each project. It will be a process or approach, but rarely a method, strictly speaking. To the outside observer, this may well be one of the most surprising aspects of the designer's *modus operandi.* Unlike professions that have laid down a specific approach, and unlike the formalized methods of "design thinking"[15] that have appeared in the design sciences, the ways in which designers trained at applied arts schools go about doing things are more than a set of continually reformulated tactics and tools. They rely on the observation of idiosyncratic behaviors, exploration of the characteristics of various materials,

15   "Design thinking" could be described as an attempt in the mid-2000s to objectify designers' approaches for other practitioners of design in engineering or marketing, or as a reiteration of the same phenomenon that emerged in the 1970s "design method" movement. For an analysis of this phenomenon, see, *inter alia,* Kimbell, 2011 and 2012, as well as Vinsel, 2012.

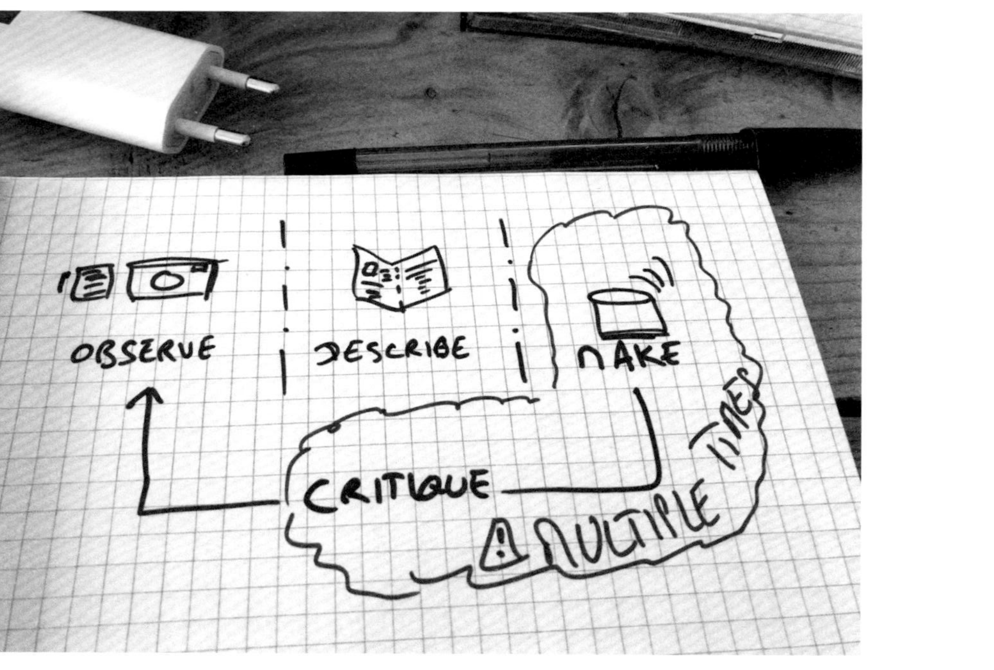

OBSERVE
DESCRIBE
MAKE
CRITIQUE
MULTIPLE TIMES

and the almost random combination of ideas and concepts to generate innovative ideas.[16] These tactics are supported by some general strategies, such as considering the problems encountered by future users and their lived contexts through participant observation, or generating ideas through action, e.g. by drawing, creating shapes out of materials or programming on a computer.

These processes, sometimes formalized at big studios, though most of the time quite spontaneous, emerge from the designers' training. After several years spent working on studio projects under the direction of one particular teacher/practitioner or another, who demonstrates and, above all, helps them understand his or her approach or sensibility through a series of activities, each designer constructs their own repertoire of tactics based on these experiences, on their own ways of doing things and on their exchanges with colleagues. One month of a designer's training may involve, for example, a week spent with a teacher demonstrating how to combine observations of social practices, interviews and modeling of design proposals; two weeks with a practitioner who seeks to repurpose an existing object to create new uses by taking it apart and hybridizing it with another; and several days of discussions based on a series of examples (posters, interfaces, products) to

16   So much so that the approach can even be playful, as proposed by the ENIAROF collective.

[Fig. 4] Example of a creative process, summarized by a designer at Nokia's design studio (2012)

be formally analyzed in order to come up with a new iteration. All this without any instruction in a single, specific, standardized method—on which the various instructors would probably have a hard time agreeing anyway.[17]

Depending on the projects, on their duration and the contexts in which they are to be used and their imperatives, these ways of doing things are combined and adapted in an *ad hoc* process that makes it possible to organize working time accordingly. This process is used to canvass for business or cost a project to be billed to the client—whether a commercial client or for the execution of a research project—but also to reach an agreement with the various parties involved. Beyond these pragmatic considerations, process thinking also requires designers to make explicit a sequencing of activities that might be regarded as being halfway between the concept of "workflow" in engineering and procedures in art. While "workflow" refers to a sequence of mutually enriching phases and loops between different periods of observation, discussion, modeling, experimen-

17   A more widespread practice at design schools is to host "process talks," during which designers recount the development of one or several projects, describing their initial impulses, process-related choices, and results, but also the pitfalls, limitations and pleasant surprises they have encountered.

18   Commonly associated with conceptual art, the concept of "protocol" in art refers to a set of rules laid down by artists for the realization of their works, as scientists do in their research work.

19   For more on these issues, see Cross, 2011.

                    Investigation/Design

ting on materials, and sketching, "procedures" in art denotes a freer, more playful combination of these stages.[18]

This process is also physically situated in the studio space. This is a context in which spatial organization—walls on which to hang things, tables on which to draw, write or amass all sorts of things, screens of all sizes—and tools—from the drawing board to the sewing machine, 3D printer (or not) and various software on our computers—are used to model, write, organize, produce presentations or renderings, but above all to share. Because the situated process set in motion by designers depends on a fundamental collective aspect. Contrary to the popular image of the solitary author, being a designer generally involves a certain sociability: working together, showing one another things (photographs or observational sketches, a prototype, a recently enjoyed novel, material samples, an inspiring poster, an online video etc.) and discussing them more or less in depth. "Design crits" are a case in point: these formalized collective sessions, sometimes with outside guests, involve confrontations of viewpoints and opinions about a project in progress (whether commercial or not), which will be sometimes painstakingly worked in and sometimes ignored, but always discussed in the course of putting the project together.

If the ways of doing design are based on this ability to think in terms of processes[19] and establish a given process to suit each project, what are the ramifications for investigative designers? Before attempting to answer this question in the next chapter, we should note that two particular aspects make for the originality of a practice-based research project: (1) The implementation of an original and innovative investigative system and process, which is as important as the end results—products or knowledge. This makes it a creation in and of itself. (2) Its temporally and spatially situated nature brings out a research context and a form of sociability that differ from those of solitary researchers or research laboratories.[20]

20   For an analysis of the situated nature of these processes, see Ricci and Allen (2020) and the special issue of the journal *Diseña* to which their article serves as the introduction.

INTEGRATION
Trained in a tradition that is disinclined to respect the boundaries and constraints of separate disciplines, designers take an all-inclusive approach to their investigations.

A second characteristic of the way in which designers—including investigative designers—go about things is that they consider all sorts of issues, references and approaches in their projects. Whether it is a matter of combining references to works (products, prototypes, publications, cultural works) in a very wide-ranging domain, or methods drawn from various disciplines (ranging from artistic processes and engineering to ethnography and the natural sciences), the processes outlined above are based on reappropriation and combination. Designers do not dwell on scruples about the potential pitfalls of such combinations, even though practitioners or researchers in the source disciplines, accustomed to more standardized procedures or a tighter focus, will sometimes raise eyebrows at such transpositions.[21] Sometimes for good reasons, but sometimes not, for it is precisely the enthusiastic spontaneity of this attitude that makes many an investigative designer's work relevant.

In other words, design involves an integrative and inclusive approach. Taking as their point of departure a context in which to operate, an object to reinvent or a general topic, designers "cast their nets wide," with an openness that seeks to take into account technical parameters, aesthetic considerations and the socio-cultural history of a given phenomenon, even if that sometimes means bringing up works of fiction, scientific discoveries or artistic projects. This is, by the way, an interesting distinction between design and another project-based discipline: engineering also avails itself of equally far-flung references—just consider the prominence of science fiction in the imaginations of engineers—but without necessarily explicitly presenting them in an ideational process, as if they were too far outside the scope of the matter at hand.[22] It seems to me that designers, whose thinking is doubtless less positivistic than engineers' thanks to their exposure to the humanities, the arts and critical thinking in their training, are less inclined to rein in their interventions in a great many areas that lie outside their creative processes. These areas allow them to wi-

21   A good example is ethnography reinterpreted as a system for field investigation preliminary to a creative project. If ethnography is taken up as a combination of observation methods and interviews, which are less commonly used than in anthropology, and without the original conceptual and methodological framework, it does nonetheless allow for various fruitful reinterpretations (cf. Nova, 2015).
22   On this question of the influence of science fiction on engineering and its pitfalls, see e.g. Bell and Dourish, 2007.

                    Investigation/Design

den the scope and ramifications of their creations. And this is what makes them unique investigators.

How does this inclusive and integrative character translate into practice? It usually widens the focus of an investigation to encompass all manner of considerations—sometimes to the detriment of the requisite specificity, especially if the project concerns a specific context or purpose. I remember one designer, for instance, who was involved in a project to reinvent protective face masks. He had amassed hundreds of photographs showing the use of face masks in real-life situations, users' gestures, the history of masks in European folklore, examples drawn from science fiction movies, as well as a whole slew of patents for highly sophisticated face masks filed by various industrialists, and the disassembly of a few masks fitted out with electronic devices which a friend of his had found on a trip to Southeast Asia. His efforts culminated in a sort of catalog. This case is an example of a wide-ranging enthusiasm that combines an analysis of gestures, fictional productions, materiality, and past and present technical and symbolic references. While his investigation was by no means exhaustive, and had no such ambition anyway, the very pragmatic inclusion of the diverse resources available to this designer strikes me as a good example of a practically oriented investigation. Whereas researchers in the social sciences would focus on a single aspect by formulating a thesis for their investigation, the thinking here is all-inclusive insofar as it is guided by a

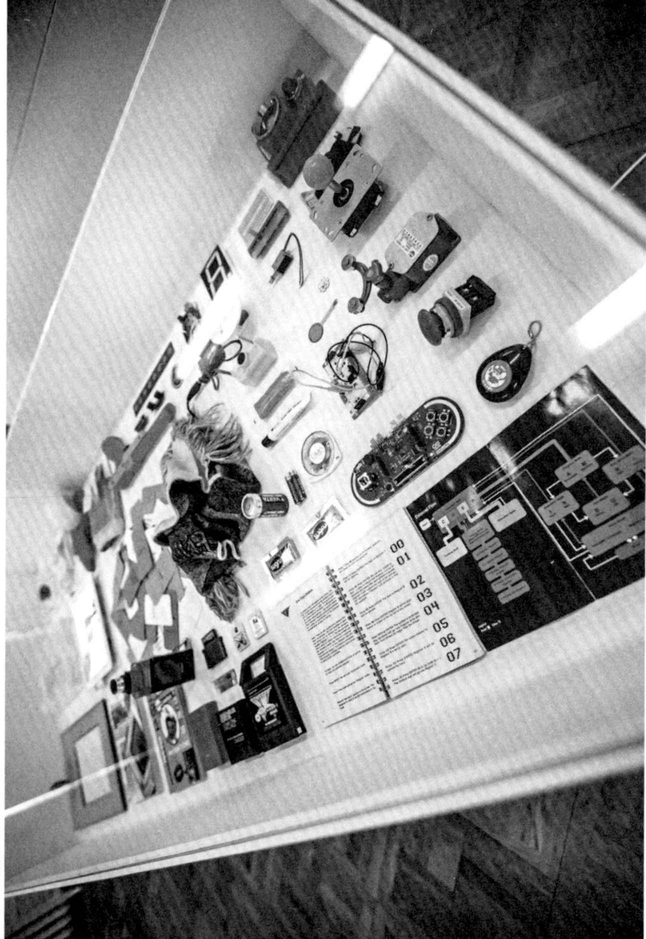

concrete objective, which consists of finding ways to shift and broaden perspectives and combine different points of view in order, first, to construct an observer's point of view that is sensitive to all sorts of different aspects, and then to create an innovative object. While fundamental to the way investigative designers work, this openness nevertheless has its limitations and drawbacks, to which I will return in the conclusion to this book.

The second characteristic feature of the wide scope of the investigative designer's approach is the *ad hoc* use of diverse methods. These methods are borrowed mostly from the social sciences and journalism. The widespread use of observation (whether participant or not) and interviewing techniques in general is combined with a vigorous use of various visual methods of producing investigative materials: observational sketches, drawings of comic strip frames, diagrams and visualizations, photographs and films. All these tools, including the designers' individual practices—whether inspired or influenced by other training or not—, are spontaneously marshaled according to the demands of the project at hand.[23] But these transfers are not confined to ethnography: witness the recent interest of designers and investigative artists in such other disciplines as forensics[24] and the empirical natural sciences.[25] If, as expounded above, the process is

[Fig. 5] *Retrocompatible Museum* (Douglas Stanley and Antonin Fourneau): an exploration of memorable products and objects in video-game culture, as a preliminary to reinventing joysticks and video games (2013)

as important as the end results, combining these methods drawn from multiple disciplines is one concrete way to reinvent one's own approach.[26]

23   It is not surprising in this regard that inductive approaches, such as anchored instruction theory (with its absence of any initial theoretical framework) or actor-network theory (which extends the networks of actors to be studied), should appeal to investigative designers, since they legitimize forms of investigation commonly practiced by designers—especially because they come close to spontaneous approaches taught by their practitioners, even though the said frameworks are often presented in design courses.

24   See e.g. Forensic Architecture's projects or "Forensic Fantasies" by the KairUs duo, who investigate data found on hard disks recovered from public dumps.

25   Fueled in particular by anthropologist Anna Lowenhaupt Tsing's "arts of noticing", which combine ethnographic inquiry and natural history (Tsing, 2017).

26   Besides those methods, a related tactic consists of mixing investigative materials of various kinds with primary and secondary sources, sometimes without any apparent awareness of the questions that such a practice raises.

In addition to their integrative, all-round aspect, the processes of investigative designers require the creation of specific tools to carry out their investigations, tools that not only tie into a specific sensibility, but are often material, rooted in the creation of dedicated artifacts or devices.

The most common example thereof is "cultural probes" (Gaver *et al.* 1999), a set of objects with which to explore a given population's customs and practices in order to discover creative opportunities. As initially proposed by its creators, who were involved in designing interfaces and technological systems, a cultural probe was a package containing postcards, envelopes, maps, a disposable camera and the kind of notebooks designers use, in which the respondents are asked to note their "impressions." The probes served to establish a connection with the respondents to a survey, in addition to or in lieu of the more traditional methods of observation and interviews.

These cultural probes were left with the respondents to elicit "inspirational responses." After using them, they'd send them back to the designers of the survey in the pre-addressed postage-paid envelopes provided. Upon receipt of the probes, the designers would use them as a source of inspiration. But the inventors of this tool stressed its broader interest: not only what it says about people's customs and practices, but also the meaning they assign to those customs and practices. Cultural probes can be used specifically to challenge or invite criticism of technologies and then to create artifacts based on the respondents' assorted views.[27] This tool eventually came to be exploited as a new means of collecting data, but the original intention was to combine the material produced with proposals reflecting the tensions, ambiguities and issues present in the probes. Over the past thirty years or so, this approach has given rise to a profusion of kits of all kinds to help inves-

27   "Unlike much research, we don't emphasize precise analyses or carefully controlled methodologies; instead, we concentrate on aesthetic control, the cultural implications of our designs, and ways to open new spaces for design. [...] Unlike most design, we don't focus on commercial products, but on new understandings of technology. [...] Instead of designing solutions for our users, we work to provide opportunities to discover new pleasures, new forms of sociability, and new cultural forms. We often act as provocateurs through our designs, trying to shift current perceptions of technology functionally, aesthetically, culturally, and even politically" (Gaver *et al.*, 1999, p. 24–25).
28   See e.g. http://www.observationalpractices.org/ and https://kit.exposingtheinvisible.org/thekit.html

tigative designers, but also sociologists and anthropologists.[28] They are used to draw up surveys addressing various topics, such as the influence of digital devices on everyday life, learning issues in collaborative situations and the affective dimension of interior design.

Another category illustrating designers' ability to create their own means of investigation concerns the profusion of data capture and recording devices that they design and utilize. *An Apparatus for Capturing Other Points of View* (2009), by my colleague Julian Bleecker, is a good example. In this project, the author revisits the work of urban sociologist William H. Whyte, who explored the use of urban spaces by filming them from above. Bleecker came up with the idea of capturing the movements of passers-by using two digital cameras mounted on a seven-meter pole. The data collected is then processed to produce a series of images, sometimes static and sometimes quite animated, revealing the mobility strategies employed by pedestrians at spots like Times Square in New York City. His aim was to find a suitable means of observing and describing practical aspects of the real world, but one that could also provide inspiration for him as a designer. What kind of knowledge does such an apparatus yield? Building on Whyte's observations, the author notes that, while pedestrian mobility seems at first glance by and large predictable, like a computer program, the apparatus makes it possible to capture plenty of exceptions.[29] And judging by these

[Fig. 6 and 7] **Creation of a device to pick up WiFi waves for the project *The Immaterials. Light Painting WiFi* (Arnall et al., 2011)**

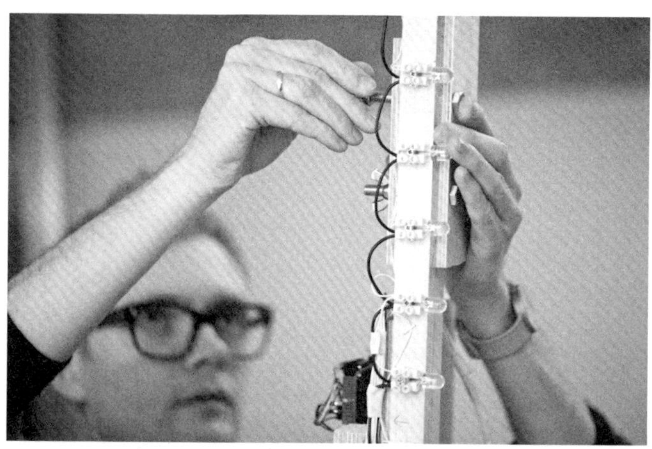

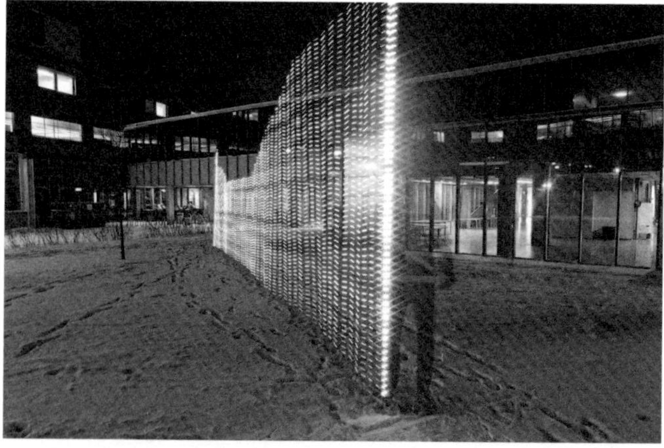

deviations from the norm, Bleecker concludes that new metaphors are needed to describe urban flows and to allow for their finer details.

The Immaterials. Light Painting WiFi by Timo Arnall and his colleagues is another striking example. As part of a research project on the material qualities of electromagnetic waves, the investigative designers used long-exposure photography at night to film a moving light rod that detects available WiFi networks. The resulting video shows how each building they pass is surrounded by a "digital envelope," thereby revealing the ubiquitous urban infrastructure that is invisible to the human eye. The object of this short film is to study the "spatial and material qualities of wireless networks" and to gain an understanding of how they are "both shaped by the environment and influence how urban spaces can be used" (Arnall *et al.*, 2013). While the video itself remains purely descriptive, the team's publications provide an analytical look at the knowledge thereby produced. By following the urban peregrinations in the film, the viewer becomes aware of inequalities in network access, for example, or the way in which private space (the WiFi network of an institution or apartment) has come to colonize public space.

But this material creativity is not confined to designing systems to yield data for investigative purposes: it can also serve in analyzing the collected material. During a course co-taught

29 See the accompanying text (Bleecker, 2009).

by his colleague Andrew van de Moere on new digital interfaces and designing urban services (Van de Moere and Hill, 2009), Dan Hill photographed a series of street scenes. The idea was to use this visual material, taking these concrete, situated cases as their point of departure, to analyze constraints on and opportunities for creativity, while avoiding simplistic visions of the cities of the future that ignore the complexity of contexts and geographies. The students analyzed the resulting photographs by affixing a sheet of tracing paper to each of them and noting the presence of digital data sources of various kinds (mobility, electricity consumption, meteorological, etc.). These graphic traces enabled them to draw up a map of this new "material," which the investigative designers then used to produce ideas for new scenarios and services based on the same hypothetically capturable data.[30]

These various examples clearly show that the ways that designers proceed, combining the process of observation and the creation of material tools, can be ways of thinking about and analyzing situations. While they can fuel a creative approach (design), they can also produce knowledge about the situation studied (design investigation).

---

30 Another striking example of "designerly thinking" in the analysis of investigative material is Shannon Mattern's analogy in her "forensic crazy walls", i.e. "evidence boards" (or walls) on which contents from various sources are pinned or pasted and connected up by a red thread for "link analysis" as in Hollywood detective movies (Mattern, 2017).

Moreover, these cases illustrate what my colleague Julian Bleecker at the Near Future Laboratory calls "observe-make-think-with-material at one time," i.e. a specific mode of reasoning based on the creation of an observational system suited to producing a description of practical reality and stimulating our understanding of a phenomenon.

Lastly, what distinguishes design-investigation
is the importance attached to the form in
which its findings are reported.

To conclude this overview of the designers' modus operandi, it is also distinguished, as a conse-
quence of their attachment to materiality, by the
form in which investigative work is reported.
Whether it's a study on the perception of electromagnetic waves (WiFi, RFID or Bluetooth) in
the form of a visual bestiary of imaginary creatures;[31] a concise cartography of our gestures reconfigured by digital tools via a print-on-demand
booklet;[32] or an analysis of controversies about
shrinking glaciers due to global warming, presented in an interactive installation that gene-
rates maps,[33] the approach is the same: the way
in which the investigation is reported is an act of
creation unto itself, which is why it is presented
in a precise format. In addition to the above examples, this list includes original forms also used
in the social sciences, such as photo books, comic
strips, fanzines, ethnography films, video mon-
tages and data displays.

These examples testify to a wide variety of formats that document the investigations "differently" and illustrate the wide range of approaches to the subjects explored by investigative designers based on the intrinsic qualities of certain media. They often choose non-textual formats—photographs, sketches, visual elements arranged to allow for comparisons—in order to elucidate matters that are difficult to express verbally. Similarly, the experiential dimension is currently writ large, e.g. projects in which exhibition-goers are invited to handle interactive devices, in order to drive home a given phenomenon through hands-on interactive experience. So the investigative designers' reasoning as embodied in these

31   Inspired by illustrated books on botany and natural history, and based on her research into the characteristics of these technologies and the anxieties users may have about them, designer Ingeborg Thomas has created a typology of electromagnetic waves depicted in the form of imaginary creatures. Each of these various radio technologies is reinterpreted and described as a perceptible phenomenon, with which various cultural representations of users' anxieties and preconceptions are associated (Thomas, 2007).

32   In the project *Curious Rituals: Gestural Interaction in the Digital Everyday* (Nova *et al.*, 2012).

33   As in *Italian Limes,* a project by the Studio Folder in Milan (Ferrari, Pasqual, Bagnato, 2018) that maps the shifting border between Austria and Italy due to the impact of global warming on the glacier that delimits that border. This interactive installation reproduces the border displacement by means of sensors located on the Alpine massif, which collect data and transmit them to an Arduino module. The module, in turn, controls a pantograph, which traces the movements of the glacier, and consequently of the international border, in real time.

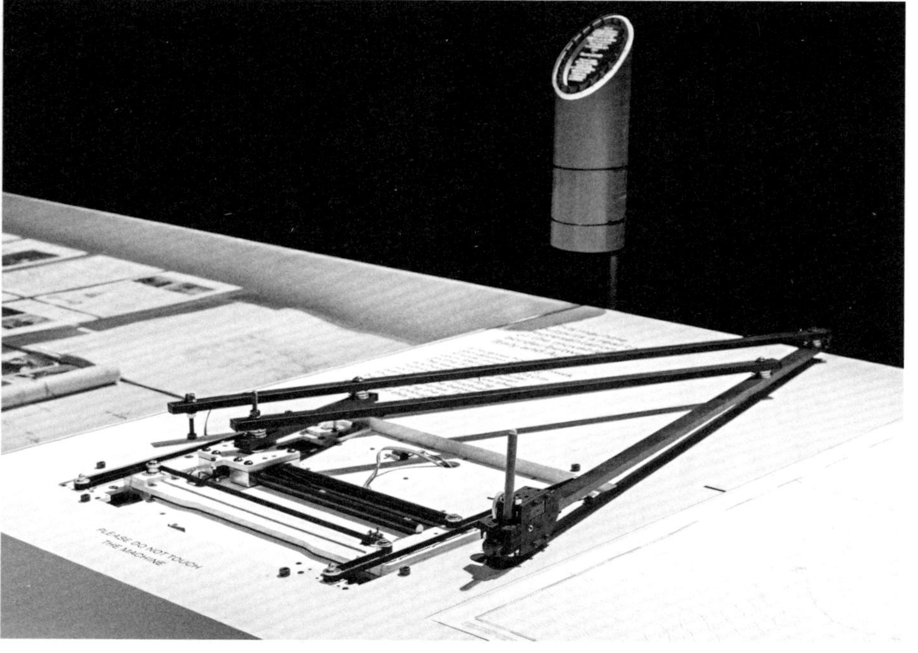

PLEASE DO NOT TOUCH
THE MACHINE

objects and devices reveals their modus operandi: it is indeed a matter of inventing forms and assemblages by playing with materials and their intrinsic properties in order to offer rich descriptions of various phenomena, or creating tangible forms with the practical aim of enabling users to perceive, read, compare and experiment.

This attention to form corresponds to a fundamental aspect of design: every act of design is an act of communication. Every design project targets a certain audience or addressee, who is rarely an expert. Historically speaking, the designer's target audience is the general public, and the designer (generally) takes special care to ensure that each project—whether for the creation of an object, poster or interface—is accessible and comprehensible to the layperson. This striving towards "audience design" translates into a combination of explanatory, even pedagogical, efforts and unusual aesthetic formats, articulated in a formal rhetoric that speaks to a community that is seldom confined to the designer's peers. The display methods Timo Arnall chose for his video representations of WiFi waves make a complex reality readily perceptible, and the installation displaying glacial movements invites exhibition-goers to discover the effects of climate change for themselves through direct observation.

[Fig. 8] *Italian Limes* (2014–2019), detail of the drawing machine part of the interactive installation presented at the 14th International Architecture Exhibition, la Biennale di Venezia. The pantograph is connected to a remote server that stores the real-time positioning data from the sensors installed on the Gräfferner glacier.

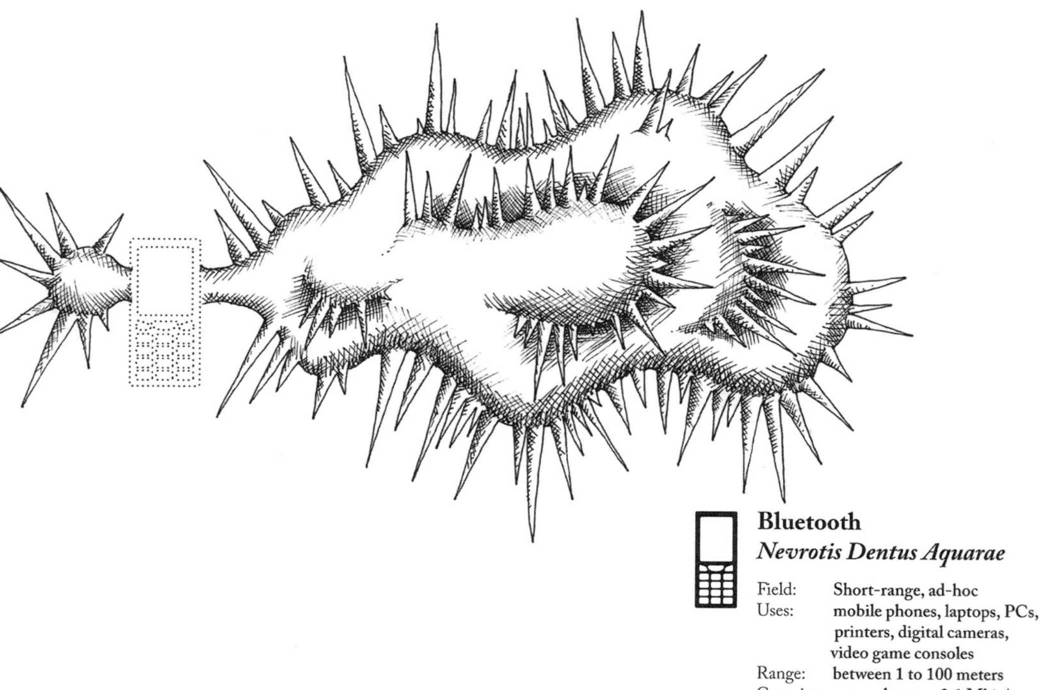

Bluetooth
Nevrotis Dentus Aquarae

Field: Short-range, ad-hoc
Uses: mobile phones, laptops, PCs,
            printers, digital cameras,
            video game consoles
Range: between 1 to 100 meters
Capacity: currently up to 2.1 Mbit/s

Furthermore, it is a matter not only of presenting aesthetically crafted "renderings" upon completion of an investigation—which remains an essential aspect—but of thinking about the investigative project in terms of form from the very outset, which will condition the entire investigative and creative process. Studying how digital devices have reconfigured human gestures by cataloging those changes in a book, for example, as I did in my *Curious Rituals* project (2012), is not the same thing as creating a series of small artifacts transcribing the gestures of smartphone use, as the designer Gabriele Meldaikyte did (2013). The choice of form influences how we produce and analyze our investigative material as well as specifying the subject or subject-matter of the investigation itself.

[Fig. 9] Bestiary of imaginary creatures to document users' representations of electromagnetic waves (in this case, Bluetooth) (Thomas, 2007)

To sum up, I began by showing the many ways in which designers become investigators in the course of their creative projects, in order to fuel and frame those projects. I also pointed out that this "creative investigation" has taken on so much importance over time that it has even become an end in itself. It leads to an approach that I call "investigative design." Investigative designers share an array of distinctive characteristics, inherited from the way designers go about things, combined with approaches drawn from the social sciences and other disciplines: namely, the importance of a continually reinvented procedural dimension, an inclusive approach that embraces a wide range of references and methods, and an emphasis on creating investigative devices out of physical material, and on unusual forms of presentation. These four characteristics testify to the originality of the designer's investigative approach.

They are not necessarily exclusive to designers. Reasoning in terms of materials, which is key to creating systems and devices for recording and organizing information, harks back to the production of measuring instruments in the history of science,[34] for example. Nor is this interest in the creation of forms limited to the natural sciences, for anthropologists nowadays sometimes fall back on such methods[35] or defend the underlying principles thereof[36]—not to mention the social sciences' recent interest in aesthetically and formally conceived presentation, e.g. using film or comics, which corresponds to this convergence as well, or the advent in the late 2000s of "sensory ethnography" to promote visual and audio forms beyond the printed text (Pink, 2009).

The investigative designer is an interesting figure for two reasons in particular. First of all, because it points up a promising path for prac-

34　For a discussion of this point, see Waquet, 2015.

35　As attested by this passage by anthropologist Claude Lévi-Strauss: "I succeeded in representing the very complex transformations I wanted to bring to light only at the end of an undertaking that was both manual and intellectual. With cardboard, paper and string, I built three-dimensional models, for many of my diagrams are only two-dimensional projections. One of these models, nearly a meter high, hung from the ceiling of the Laboratory for Social Anthropology like a Calder mobile for several months until it fell apart." *De près et de loin, Conversations avec Claude Lévi-Strauss* (Eribon, 1991).

36　This is what Tim Ingold proposes: "Could certain practices of art, for example, suggest new ways of doing anthropology? If there are similarities between the ways in which artists and anthropologists study with the world, then could we not regard the artwork as a result of something like an anthropological study, rather than as an object of such study?" (Ingold, 2013, p. 9).

tice-based research in design, following on from the conduct of surveys—a means of producing knowledge which I think designers in search of academic legitimacy ought to be acquainted with or reminded of. But also because this approach is part of a broader context that goes beyond design: namely the debate between the "creative social sciences," which seek to invent novel and unique modes of representation of social phenomena,[37] and the growing interest in investigation in artistic fields like contemporary art[38] and literature.[39] In the wake of film, photography and literature, design is thus positioning itself as another key agent of renewal for the scientific world. The growing importance of field research also attests to the emergence of new avenues for research and the budding prospects for a type of design that moves away from creating everyday objects.[40] It also brings us back to the question of the knowledge produced by these creative investigations, what Francesca Cozzolino calls "sensitive knowledge,"

37   As a follow-up to the debate about experimentation in ethnographic writing that was sparked by the publication of *Writing Culture* (Clifford & Marcus, 1986) or more broadly as part of current efforts to decompartmentalize "science and the arts" (Becker, 2009; Debaene, 2010; Jablonka, 2014).

38   On the figure of the investigative artist, see Foster, 1996, and a critical rereading thereof in Duperrex, 2019. See also Kreplak *et al*, 2011.

39   For an overview of this subject, see Demanze, 2019.

40   A movement similar to what occurs in collaboration between designers and humanities researchers in the field of digital humanities (Burdick *et al.*, 2012; Masure, 2017).

in order to materialize the processes and practices that turn art and design into sensitive knowledge of a new kind (Cozzolino, 2017).

While the applied arts are renewing field investigations, its practices and objectives, a major challenge remains: How do we conduct rigorous investigations? How are we to assess the quality of an investigation? Let us reiterate here that the processes underlying these investigations, like the methodology of research endeavors in the natural and social sciences, are just as important as reporting on the findings. The investigative designer's processes depend on the choice of a set of hypotheses or constraints—including specified observation procedures and forms of rendering and presentation—that can be made explicit, e.g. by specifying the sources of theoretical, methodological or artistic inspiration on which they are based. The examples described above are cases in point: Julian Bleecker's project is not the upshot of a sudden, spontaneous choice, for it is about reinterpreting a sociological study and capitalizing on cutting-edge technology to reformulate that study in a revealing way. The above-mentioned bestiary of imaginary creatures as an allegorical portrayal of the invasive omnipresence of electromagnetic waves is based on the history of the bestiary as a situated form of knowledge and on its choice of forms as a means of elucidating moral issues, much the way fantastical creatures were employed for moralizing purposes in the Middle Ages. These two investigations by designers draw their epistemic validity in large measure from the fact that they form part of a specific intellectual trajectory and offer well-reasoned arguments for their creative choices. However, this is not always the case. The methodological, scientific and artistic references and analogies underlying many of these projects remain tacit or are described, if at all, only within the investigating team. Investigative designers would be well advised to make them explicit if they wish to underscore the epistemic quality of their work. The analogical reasoning underlying their work is a key element of its rigor—always provided that it is made plain.

Lastly, it should be stressed that the existence and growing appeal of these projects does not mean they can do without any accompanying text: the means of production, analysis and presentation of investigation materials are, as a rule, complementary. Design creations as "intermediate objects" are enriched by a written exposition of the designer's choices with regard to the four aspects discussed above. Absent such a text, we are liable to find ourselves faced with a spontaneous investigation that may well be interesting and unusual, but insufficiently elucidated for a peer assessment of its conceptual and analytical rigor.

 Investigation/Design

THE FUTURE OF
CREATIVE INVESTIGATION

The advent of investigative design[41] comes at an opportune time, for its approach corresponds to new questions, debates and currents in research in the humanities and social sciences. Without attempting an exhaustive treatment that would go beyond the scope of these concluding remarks, it would seem relevant to point out two promising paths for practice-based research.

Creative-investigative approaches are particularly relevant to fields of study that are related to digital technologies and cultures. In the first instance, because information and communication technologies are one means of revitalizing historical, sociological, literary and geographic investigation. But also because several current fields of research make use of them: in particular, the "digital humanities," which draw on digital resources and analytical and display tech-

---

41 One recent development involves new education programs like the Design Investigation Studio at Die Angewandte in Vienna: https://designinvestigations.at/

nologies, among other things, to revolutionize approaches to history, linguistics, archaeology and art history.[42] Likewise, computational social science is enriching the methods of sociological inquiry with tools for collecting, processing and displaying digital data in order to understand, analyze and model social phenomena. Also worth mentioning in this regard is media archaeology, which studies new and emerging media, such as smartphones and smart speakers, by examining precursors, however curious or strange they may be, to nuance the received view of history as one of linear evolutionary continuity.

These three fields, although distinct in terms of their hypotheses and theoretical frameworks, constitute suitable testing grounds for the forms of creative investigation discussed in this book. One important aspect of their approaches is indeed combining investigation techniques, the exploration of materials, and forms of presentation that are accessible and shareable even outside research communities, e.g. by using data displays, unusual formalizations and interactive devices. For, although researchers in the humanities and social sciences are equipped with conceptual, historical, reflective and methodological tools, their

42   Among the myriad projects of this kind, see e.g. *Terra Forma: Manuel de cartographies potentielles* (Aït-Touati *et al.*, 2019), the *Critical Zones* exhibition at the ZKM (Latour and Weibel, 2020) and *Feral Atlas* (Tsing *et al.*, 2020).
43   Following on in particular from the work and propositions of researchers like Donna Haraway (2020) and Anna Tsing (2017).

                    Investigation/Design

relation to the creation of processes or forms of presentation, and more broadly to the construction of a point of view rooted in a material practice, doesn't always live up to the ambitions of the three fields in question. This is where the investigative designer's expertise and know-how can enrich their approaches.

A second promising domain for the forms of creative investigation presented here is "Anthropocene studies," an interdisciplinary field looking into human influence past and present on the geology and biology of planet Earth. Recent years have seen the emergence of a great many works at the confluence of the social and natural sciences that bear directly on the environment, from anthropology to ecology and geography, on the one hand, and design or art, on the other. So these two creative fields of endeavor are often called in to revamp or redesign scientific approaches in these academic disciplines—and to heighten our awareness of the world, our attention and sensitivity to it, to broaden our perspectives and reinvigorate our understanding of it.[43] But these fields also seek to understand the world through sensitive, unusual and purpose-built forms.

Depending on the project, this may go in three different directions. First, it may involve new ways of documenting the world and its upheavals, as in the aforementioned *Italian Lime* project (cf. Fig. 8) or the many "citizen science projects" and other participant inquiries that seek to enable lay volunteers to describe and understand environmental changes (global warming, loss of biodiversity, pollution).

A second axis concerns the materialization of scenarios and possible trajectories, presented in the form of speculative design or "design fiction" projects. A case in point is the projects of design students at Die Angewandte (University of Applied Arts Vienna) addressing future lifestyles and human-environmental relations in the Austrian Alps in the medium term, based on inquiries into the past and present practices of mountain populations.[44] The aim of this speculative work is to go beyond mere description or prediction in order to mull over imaginary scenarios and rethink our relationship to the environment.

The third axis more specifically concerns investigations carried out by designers in contact with other disciplines and oriented towards interventions, i.e. designing services, architecture, products, interfaces or town and country planning with a view to addressing and, ideally, mitigating environmental issues.

In these three areas, as in research currents related to digital technologies and cultures, investigative design is all the more relevant since some of these endeavors seek to broaden views that have historically been too reductionist and take a constructive and participatory approach to the issues involved, which are all too often left to spe-

44 Discussed in the book *After Abundance: A Speculation on Climate Change in the Alps,* by Anab Jain and Thomas Geisler (2018).

              Investigation/Design

cialists. Investigative designers' know-how and broad, inclusive points of view make for presentations of investigative findings that say more to a lay public, so they can provide invaluable tools for a necessary—and duly nuanced—reflection on environmental issues. They can produce knowledge or take action through concrete projects.

Thanks to Laurence Allard, Anne Bationo-Tillon, Julian Bleecker, Anaïs Bloch, Mathilde Bourrier, Samuel Bianchini, Stefana Broadbent, Anne Burdick, Jan Chipchase, Loup Cellard, Francesca Cozzolino, Jérôme Denis, Matthieu Duperrex, Antoine Fenoglio, Nick Foster, Ramy Fischler, Jean-Louis Fréchin, Christophe Guignard, Fabien Girardin, Yves Grassioulet, Etienne Guerry, Dan Hill, Cornelia Hummel, Patrick Keller, Lysianne Léchot-Hirt, Anab Jain, Timothée Jobert, Claudia Mareis, Anthony Masson, Anthony Masure, Anna Meroni, Alexandra Midal, Alexandre Monnin, Emanuele Quinz, Justin Pickard, Donato Ricci, Mirweis Sangin, Mark Vanderbeeken, Stéphane Vial, Beatrice Villari, Olivier Wathelet, Basile Zimmerman et Jan-Christoph Zoels… for all the discussions we had about the points addressed in this essay. Special thanks again to Francesca and Lysianne for proofreading and constructive comments on the manuscript.

Greetings to all the students in the Media Design master's program at HEAD – Genève, the course in Artistic Practices at the École Polytechnique Fédérale de Lausanne, the Design Investigations program at Die Angewandte (Vienna), the Service Design master's program at the Politecnico di Milano, ENSCI Les Ateliers (Paris) and the master's program in Media Design Practice at the Art Center College of Design (Los Angeles), with whom I've been working on these approaches for over ten years.

Aït-Touati, F., Arènes, A. and Grégoire, A., *Terra Forma : Manuel de cartographies potentielles,* Paris, B42, 2019

Arnall, T., Knutsen, J. and Martinussen, E. S., "Immaterials : Light painting WiFi," in *Significance,* vol. 10, no 4, 2013

Arnall, T., Martinussen, E. S. and Knutsen, J., *The Immaterials. Light Painting WiFi,* 2011, https://vimeo.com/20412632

Becker, H., *Telling About Society,* London and Chicago, The University of Chicago Press, 2007

Bell, G. and Dourish, P., "Yesterday's tomorrows: notes on ubiquitous computing's dominant vision," in *Personal and Ubiquitous Computing,* vol. 11, no 2, 2007

Berthelot, J.-M., *Épistémologie des sciences sociales,* Paris, Presses universitaires de France, 2001

Bleecker, J., « William H. Whyte Revisited. An Experiment with an Apparatus for Capturing Other Points of View », in Near Future Laboratory Blog, 2009, blog.nearfuturelaboratory. com/2009/08/10/an-apparatus-for-capturing-other-points-of-view/

Burdick, A., Drucker, J., Lunenfeld, P., Presner, T. and Schnapp, J., *Digital_Humanities,* Cambridge, MIT Press, 2012

Bianchini, S., "From Instrumental Research in Art to its Sharing: Producing a commons, respecting the singular," in *Transdisciplinary & Interdisciplinary Education and Research, The ATLAS,* (ed. H. Dieleman, B. Nicolescu et A. Ertas), Lubbock, Texas, 2017

Cozzolino, F., "Quand le sensible performe le réel. Gestes, pratiques et formes de la création en train de se faire," in *Les Revenants. Constellation du Tout Monde,* (ed. E. Spiesse), Bordeaux, MC2A, 2017

Cross, N., *Designerly Ways of Knowing,* Basel, Birkhäuser, 2007

Cross, N., *Design Thinking: Understanding How Designers Think and Work,* Berg Publishers, 2011

Debaene, V., *L'adieu au voyage. L'ethnologie française entre science et littérature,* Paris, Gallimard, 2010

Demanze, L., *Un Nouvel Âge de l'enquête,* Paris, José Corti, 2019

Duperrex, M., *Arcadies altérées. Territoires de l'enquête et*

          Investigation/Design

vocation de l'art en Anthropocène, PhD Thesis in Visual arts, Université de Toulouse – Jean Jaurès, 2018

Duperrex, M., "L'artiste enquêteur et les risques de la translation. Une relecture de Hal Foster," in *Litter@ Incognita,* Toulouse, Université de Toulouse Jean Jaurès, no 11, "L'œuvre comme enquête/l'enquête dans l'œuvre : création et réception," 2019

Ferrari, M., Pasqual, E. and Bagnato, A., *A Moving Border. Alpine Cartographies of Climate Change,* Ithaca, Cornell University Press, 2018

Findeli, A., "La recherche en design, questions épistémologiques et méthodologiques," in *La critique en design. Contribution à une anthologie,* (ed. F. Jollant-Kneebone), Nîmes, Jacqueline Chambon, 2003

Findeli, A. and Bousbaci, R., "L'éclipse de l'objet dans les théories du projet en design," 6th International Conference of the European Academy of Design, Bremen, 2005

Findeli, A., "Searching for Design Research Questions: Some Conceptual Clarifications," in *Questions, hypotheses & conjectures* (ed. R. Chow, W. Jonas et G. Joost), Bloomington, iUniverse, 2010

Foster, H., *The Return of the Real: The Avant-Garde at the End of the Century,* Cambridge, MIT Press, 1996

Gaver, B., Dunne, T. and Pacenti, E., "Design: Cultural probes," in *interactions,* vol. 6, no 1, 1999

Haraway, D. J., *Staying with the Trouble,* Durham and London, Duke University Press, 2016

Hill, D., "The Incomplete City," in *Medium,* 2016

Ingold, T., *Design Anthropology is not and cannot be Ethnography,* Research Network for Design Anthropology, seminar 2, Interventionist Speculations, Copenhagen, 13-14 August 2014

Ingold, T., *Making: Anthropology, Archaeology, Art and Architecture,* London, Routledge, 2013

Jablonka, I., *L'histoire est une littérature contemporaine. Manifeste pour les sciences sociales,* Paris, Seuil, 2014

Jain, A. and Geisler, T., *After Abundance: A Speculation on Climate Change in the Alps,* Basel, Birkhäuser, 2019

Kimbell, L., "Rethinking Design Thinking: Part I," in *Design and Culture,* vol. 3, no 3, p. 285-306, 2011

Kimbell, L., "Rethinking Design Thinking: Part II," in *Design and Culture,* vol. 4, no 2, 2012

Koskinen, I., Zimmerman, J., Binder, T., Redstrom, J. *et al., Design Research through Practice: From the Lab, Field, and Showroom,* Morgan Kaufmann, 2011

Kreplak, Y., Tangy, L. and Turquier, B., "Art contemporain et sciences humaines : usages réciproques," in *Tracés,* 2011, https://journals.openedition.org/traces/5234

Latour, B. and Weibel, P., *Critical Zones, The Science and Politics of Landing on Earth,* Cambridge, MIT Press, 2020

Léchot Hirt, L., *Recherche-création en design. Modèles pour une pratique expérimentale,* Geneva, Métis Presses, 2010

Lévi-Strauss, C. and Eribon, D., *De près et de loin,* Paris, Odile Jacob, 1988

Masure, A., *Design et humanités numériques,* Paris, B42, 2017

Mattern, S., "Bldg my fall Data/Archive/Infrastructure class," in *Twitter,* 2017, https://twitter.com/shannonmattern/status/895269708773150721

Van de Moere, A. and Hill, D., "Research through Design in the Context of Teaching Urban Computing," in *Proceedings of Australian Computer-Human Interaction Special Interest Group (OZCHI 2009 Conference), Street Computing Workshop,* 2009, https://lirias.kuleuven.be/retrieve/358191

Naegele, I. and Baur, R., *Scents of the City,* Zurich, Lars Müller Publishing, 2004

Nova, N., *Beyond Design Ethnography: How Designers Practice Ethnographic Research,* Berlin, SHS Publishing, 2014

Nova, N., Miyake, K., Kwon, N. and Chiu, W., *Curious Rituals: Gestural Interaction in the Digital Everyday,* Venice CA, NFL Press, 2012

Olivier de Sardan, J.-P., *La rigueur du qualitatif. Les contraintes empiriques de l'interprétation socio-anthropologique,* Louvain-la-Neuve, Academia-Bruylant (Prospective anthropology), 2008

Pink, S., *Doing Sensory Ethnography,* London, SAGE, 2009

Potter, N., *What is a designer: things, places, messages,* London, Hyphen Press, 2002

     Investigation/Design

Renucci, F. and Réol, J.-M. (ed.), "L'Artiste, un chercheur pas comme les autres," in *Hermès, La Revue,* no 72, 2015

Ricci, D. and Allen, J., "Testing Against the World," in *Diseña,* (16), 2020

Simon, H., *The Sciences of the Artificial,* Cambridge, MIT Press, 1969

Thomas, I. M. D., "Bubbles of radio," in *immelie,* 2007, http://immelie.files.wordpress.com/2007/12/project-documentation_screen.pdf

Tsing, A., Deger, J., Keleman, A. and Zhou, F., *Feral Atlas. The More-Than-Human Anthropocene,* Palo Alto, Stanford University Press, 2020

Tsing, A., *The Mushroom at the End of the World. On the Possibility of Life in Capitalist Ruins,* Princeton, Princeton University Press, 2015

Vial, S., "De la spécificité du projet en design : une démonstration," in *Communication et organisation,* vol. 46, 2014

Vinck, D., "De l'objet intermédiaire à l'objet-frontière. Vers la prise en compte du travail d'équipement," in *Revue d'anthropologie des connaissances,* vol. 3, no 1, 2009, https://www.cairn.info/

Vinsel, L., "Design Thinking Is a Boondoggle," in *Chronicle Review,* 2018, https://www.chronicle.com/article/Design-Thinking-Is-a/243472

Waquet, F., *L'ordre matériel des savoirs. Comment les savants travaillent (XVIe -XXIe siècles),* Paris, CNRS, 2015

Whyte, W., *The Social Life of Small Urban Spaces,* Washington D.C., The Conservation Foundation, 1980

HEAD – Publishing, 2021

Texts published under free
license CC BY–SA

Title: *Investigation/Design,*
(original title: *Enquête /
Création en design*)

Author: Nicolas Nova

Manifestes collection edited
by Julie Enckell Julliard and
Anthony Masure

Editorial coordinator: Sylvain
Menétrey

Translation: Walter Hackman

Proofreading: Stephanie O'Dea

Manifestes collection
designed by Dimitri Broquard

Fonts: ABC Whyte (Dinamo,
2019), Lyon Text (Commercial
Type, 2009)

Printed by Artgraphic
Cavin SA

ISBN: 978-2-940510-50-4

Legal deposit: March 2021

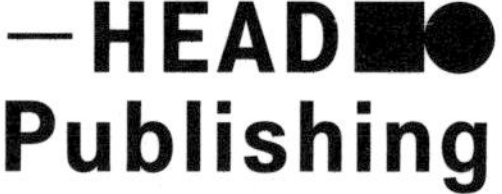

 Colophon

[Fig. 1.]: Photo: Anaïs Bloch
[Fig. 2.]: Photo: Nicolas Nova
[Fig. 3.]: © HEAD – Genève,
    photo : Michel Giesbrecht
[Fig. 4.]: Photo: Nicolas Nova
[Fig. 5.]: Photo: Douglas
    Edric Stanley
[Fig. 6.]: Photo: Einar Sneve
    Martinussen, Jørn Knutsen
    & Timo Arnall, 2011
[Fig. 7.]: Photo: Einar Sneve
    Martinussen, Jørn Knutsen
    & Timo Arnall, 2011
[Fig. 8.]: © Studio Folder,
    photo: Delfino Sisto Legnani
[Fig. 9.]: Photo: Ingeborg
    Marie Thomas

Nicolas Nova is an associate professor at
HEAD – Genève, where he teaches Anthropology
of Digital Cultures, Ethnography and Design
Research. He is also a co-founder of the Near Future
Laboratory, a foresight and innovation agency
involved in design fiction projects. Nova explores
the uses and repurposing of technical objects in
the digital world from a socio-anthropological
perspective. He holds PhDs in the social sciences
(University of Geneva) and computer science (École
Polytechnique Fédérale de Lausanne) and has
served as visiting professor at the ArtCenter College
of Design (Pasadena, California) and Politecnico
di Milano.

Nova is the author of *Smartphones. Une
enquête anthropologique* (Métis presses, 2020),
*Beyond Design Ethnography: How Designers
Practice Ethnographic Research* (SHS Publishing,
2014), *Futurs? La panne des imaginaires techno-
logiques* (Les Moutons électriques, 2014).